Captive Spirit

By
Ron Kendrick

ACKNOWLEDGEMENTS

I would like to extend my gratitude to Ian and Margaret Petley for their encouragement and support throughout this journey.

ABOUT THE AUTHOR

This memoir has been attempted several times in the last fifty years, and then left on the shelf, until the next inspiring incident occurred or when he felt confident enough to express himself so others could understand.

The rest of his working life was as a self-employed carpenter, learning all aspects of house building from the ground up, to the roof line. Mainly specialising in kitchen installation and all home improvements .

Now with time on his hands he can explore other pursuits .

CHAPTER 1
START OF THE JOURNEY

There it was, on time, the 101 bus to Piccadilly, Manchester. It was early morning, and I was travelling to my new career, although I didn't know it at the time. Reading the Daily Mirror on the top deck and casually noting the runners for that day, Foggy Bell jumped out at me, although it was running in a flat race. I knew I had to have a bet on him.

"He will win his next race; have a bet on the nose," said my local butcher the previous year.

I walked from Piccadilly to Bury New Road, an unfamiliar area of Manchester to me, but soon found my way to Strangeways Prison. A high wall of imposing brick separated and joined by impressive turret-shaped buildings on either side of enormous double gates with a personnel door for easy access. It only took one knock, and the door opened. A man in uniform and a knowing smile checked my letter of acceptance for an interview and led me to a room just inside and to the left of what looked like a portcullis. Four other applicants were nervously pretending to read the prison regulation handbook, so I did the same.

We were all escorted through the portcullis, the same size and dimensions as the main gates, across a road and then a concrete bridge to the main entrance and into another waiting room. I was third to be

1

interviewed and took a moment to compose myself prior to answering their questions. I assumed I was doing well until some of the questions were deliberately aggressive and completely unrealistic. I instinctively knew that my patience was being tested, so I answered sensibly and politely. Who in their right mind would take a prisoner to be prepared for the gallows when the law of the land prevails along with the prison regulation handbook above the orders of the Governor. This was 1969, after all, and I said I would refuse. Other senseless questions were asked, and I remained silent with an expression that conveyed my "knowing".

"Come back after lunch for the literacy, numeracy and intelligence tests", said one of the interviewees. I knew that if I passed, I would be accepted for training.

At lunchtime, I went out of the gate to the local betting shop and put five bob each way on Foggy Bell, I should have put it on the nose, caution being my watchword.

The tests in the afternoon were simple and straightforward, sailing through them so easily that I became a little suspicious that I was being lured into the prison Service as if the path was being cleared of obstacles for me instead of me seeing them and clearing them with my own efforts.

I collected my winnings from the bookies and strolled to the bus stop in Piccadilly, the bus arriving at the same time as myself. I sat on the top deck, read the rest of the Daily Mirror, completed the crossword and wondered why the day had gone so well.

There was no effort involved that day; everything just flowed. I was aware, alert, confident and calm.

I never had a clear idea of what I wanted to do with my life. Too short for the police but I wanted a steady job as I was getting married later that year.

"Why don't you join the prison service", enthused Harry", an old school pal.

"If you can't catch the crooks, then maybe you can contain them,"

So, I applied for the job with no idea of what it would entail.

CHAPTER 2
ACCEPTED FOR TRAINING

Attend Strangeways for initial training in preparation for ongoing training at Wakefield Officers Training School, stated the letter of acceptance.

Four weeks at Strangeways, for starters, making notes of prison routine, whereabouts of fire buckets (considered essential), the position of alarm bells and other things of importance, such as where was the officer's mess and how to get there without any pass keys. Mostly observational notes, with minor insights as to the attitudes, expectations and cooperation between staff and prisoners. The routines and rules that ran the prison. I wore my civilian clothes and felt like an outsider looking in on a regime, a well-ordered society that had stood the test of decades of routine. The first thing that hits you is the stench, an almost unbearable stink that stuck to your clothes as prisoners 'slopped out' first thing in the morning. Carrying plastic pots with loose-fitting lids filled with human shit and piss. Over a thousand of them all at once. That was the odour of prison life, a humiliating and degrading experience for all involved.

Everyone, staff and prisoners, appeared to know what they were doing and doing it with endless regularity, even allowing for mishaps and mistakes that melted into the routines seamlessly. Everything was new to me, and every experience left an impression, not always visible, sometimes memorable and often wished forgettable. Four weeks went quickly as I noted the locations of fire buckets in my training manual.

The train to Wakefield Station had a corridor and was a very enjoyable journey; seeing the countryside and being able to wander the train was great. The school was modern, in its own grounds, surrounded by grass and a few trees, with a large car park adjacent to the main entrance with excellent sports facilities. Officers Training School: if successful, I would be an officer, not a warder but an officer. Had a ring of kudos.

After registration and a tour of the school, I met my roommate Johnny Morgan a solid guy who played hooker for a team in Bradford; rugby league couldn't be helped, so we got on O.K. Whenever he spoke, it was with humour and a distinctive accent, everything was funny when he was around. If you've played hooker in any of the codes, the first thing you do when you scrum down is to punch your opponent. If he punches you back, then game on; if not, then you had an easier game. Getting in first was his way of playing.

The routine before breakfast was to be on parade at a ridiculous time of the morning. Being taught to march was part of the discipline of the day. Johnny had the ability to march with his left arm and his left leg moving forward at the same time and then his right arm and right leg. I thought he was doing it on purpose, but not so; he was unable to change his way of marching; even when walking normally, he had the same gait. Started the day with a smile and made us all relax a little. Later understood it to be tick-tocking.

After breakfast we had lessons, learning about the judicial system and the power of judges with some of the history of how justice evolved to the present day.

We had weekends off and could either stay or travel home and return on Monday morning. I often travelled home but stayed one weekend to see what it was like. Should have gone home as I was not into socialising and was finding it difficult to hide my shyness.

The course was comprehensive and thorough, although I had nothing to compare it with, except perhaps school six years earlier. We covered most aspects of law from Magistrates courts and the processes that led to sentencing. Assize courts and Quarter Sessions, Criminal and Civil courts, Royal Courts of Justice, and the Appeal Court.

We also learned about category A, B, and C prisons, open prisons, experimental prisons, remand centres, borstals, and detention centres, plus a little about foreign prison systems. Also what prisoner's rights were and what were privileges.

A lot of sport was played in our spare time, basketball, football, rugby, volleyball, and badminton. Judo and self-defence were practiced every day as part of the curriculum.

Towards the end of the course, each trainee was faced with several angry protesters attacking them from all angles, and even though each attack was one at a time, several injuries were suffered by attackers and defenders. Some became overzealous; a broken arm was the worst injury, but bruises and black eyes were common, along with dislocations and strained muscles.

On one occasion, we were learning about restraints, handcuffs and straight jackets, which were still used in prisons of the day. Some of the outdated means of immobilising prisoners were on display and a volunteer was asked to be placed into a wide leather belt fitted around the waist with metal wrist clamps at either side of the body. Johnny was suddenly propelled forward, pushed by someone holding a grudge.

"Thank you for being a brave volunteer" was the response by the tutor and two of us were asked to put him in the restraints.

He had nowhere to run, but we couldn't even get the belt around his waist never mind his wrists in the clamps.

He fought like a rugby player. Exhausted, we gave up. "This is how you do it," said the tutor and he and another teacher got hold of Johnny and managed to remove his shoes; grabbing a big toe and threatening to twist it, he had him quietened down enough to put him in the restraints. It was still a real struggle, but it worked.

The training was intense, three months of learning and a lot of fun, plus making new friends and a sense of achievement when told we had passed. I'd asked to be posted to a borstal close to my hometown. I did understand that if I was married, then a posting to your local prison was 'on the cards', but if single, then it was more likely that a London Nick would be your new home. The administration knew that I was getting married in August, soon after the course finished, and so my request for a local posting would be looked on favourably.

A.M. On the penultimate day, the whole class participated in a five-mile run. I was never a runner unless racing to catch a rugby ball or a bus. Running for no reason was unreasonable, but I couldn't get out of it no matter how hard I tried.

I had a stitch within a hundred yards, heavy breathing and a headache, along with tired legs and a tremendous desire to give up. I asked myself why the other runners looked to be enjoying the jaunt. I kept up with the pace for about two miles, and as nausea began to take over, everything oddly became a little bit easier: my breathing was not as heavy, my aching legs became less painful, and the headache disappeared. The stitch disappeared as I overtook stragglers and ran with the bunch. I then went in front with a feeling of ease and confidence beyond any experience of running. I was first back at the school and the first to notice an 'apparent' accident had occurred in the main car park. A coach had seemingly careered into a vehicle, and injured passengers were alighting seeking help. As luck would have it, the cavalry arrived to administer first aid. This was the final test to see how we coped in an emergency, and surprisingly, my newfound confidence resulted in my passing with 'flying colours'.

Wandsworth Prison was to be my place of work. The day I received the posting, Johnny showed me the Daily Mirror with a front-page photo of Knifeman Frankie Frazer, better known as Mad Frankie Fraser, throwing slates from a roof at prison staff.

"But where is it?" I asked anxiously.

"That's the toughest nick in the country. It's in London, and I'm posted to Brixton".

I made a request to the powers that be for a change of posting and was advised to serve my twelve-month probationary period at Wandsworth and then apply for a transfer. I would be a responsible officer with experience and more likely to get a favourable transfer at the time. All things considered I had been selected for Wandsworth because of my capabilities, my willingness to learn and my adaptability. Well, that's what they told me, how gullible was I. My fiancé was not impressed but accepted the situation with an air of resigned good humour.

CHAPTER 3
FIRST IMPRESSIONS

Timing is everything; the course finished on the 15th of August. I was married on the 23rd, a week's honeymoon in Morecambe and then travelled to London on 2nd September and reported to the main gate of Wandsworth.

The Principal Officer in charge of training a rotund, humourless man with an ambling gait and a sneering expression, which I assumed he thought gave him a sense of authority. After being introduced to him I was then fitted out with a uniform.

- Two tunics. Navy
- Two pairs of trousers. Navy
- Two separate collared shirts. Pale blue
- Four separate collars.
- Two sets of collar stud
- A full-length raincoat.
- A heavy Great Coat.
- A whistle.
- A truncheon.
- A warrant card.
- A peaked hat.

"This is an address about a hundred yards from here, where you will be staying until further notice. The digs are approved by the Prison, you will be sharing with another recruit from your training school," sneered the P.O.

I was told to go straight there, change into my uniform and report back within the hour. Everything was a good fit, but I struggled with the shirt and separate collar. I foolishly thought I could put the studs in whilst wearing the shirt. Not so, and I stubbornly tried for about fifteen minutes; the front stud was easy, but the rear one was impossible. I eventually took the shirt off, fitted the rear stud to the collar, put the shirt on again and affixed the front stud. I was beginning to panic at the thought of being late.

Rushed back to the nick about twenty minutes late. Given a chain, a pass key and a cell key attached them to my belt. The P.O. looked at his wristwatch, tutted, and, without saying a word, gave me a tour. It was built along the same structural lines as Strangeways. I was beginning to see the vastness of it; unlike Strangeways, this was to be my place of work for the next twelve months. The similarities were uncanny as I noticed the same layout and the same staff with the same prisoners, and the same routines with the same workshops, the same kitchens. The lingering stench was the same, the entrance was the same, and the cathedral like space for lost souls was the same.

Almost everything was grey, the walls, the stone floors, the prisoner's uniforms and their pallor, the huge windows at the end of each wing. A wing has four floors: a basement called the ones, the ground floor the twos, third floor the threes and the fourth floor; you guessed it, the fours. There are five wings encircling a central hub from where a view of each wing and landing can be observed at the same time. That central position was the control and observation centre for the whole prison, with a huge cast iron patterned grill embedded in the floor overlooking the food serving area underneath. With a vista of the whole prison and the ability to see the full height all the way to the ever-present pigeons at the apex of the roof crapping on whoever was unfortunate enough to be beneath them at the time.

During my tour, I was the butt of some jibes from inmates and staff alike, my uniform being new and pristine, receiving wolf whistles and 'come on' glances. I was a little self-conscious but brushed them off with disdain.

Reunited with some mates from the same course who'd been there a whole week, brimming with confidence and considered veterans already knowing everything. Grimes, Irvine, Jones, Knowles, Kendrick, and Lomax took me a few hours to figure it out. All were pre-selected according to our specific interests, abilities and intelligence for such a high-security establishment like Wandsworth. Mason, Mitchell, Pearce and Richards were posted to Brixton Prison. Those whose names began with A, B, C, D, E, and F were probably serving at Wormwood Scrubs or Pentonville. I decided not to make any representations or create any discourse until after my probation was successful.

Tuesday morning at 6.45 am, I collected my cell key and passkey and met with the rest of the staff at the main entrance; only I and my 'veteran' buddies produced our truncheons, warrant cards and whistles. Orders of the day were issued; each landing was then manned by two Discipline officers (D.O.s). Each wing office located on the twos was manned by a Principal Officer (P.O.) and Senior officer (S.O.)

CHAPTER 4
FIRST FULL DAY

My first action was to count the prisoners on my side of the landing, shout that number to the wing P.O., who then added all the numbers from his wing and reported to the Centre P.O., who checked all the numbers from all the wings and if they tallied with the overnight total would order an unlock. This only took about ten minutes. Prisoners can be observed through a spyglass with a hinged plate on the outside of the door at about eye level.

Usually, half of each landing was unlocked at a time for the inmates to carry out their plastic pots full of shit and piss and along with their embarrassment and flush it down the sluices. They would return to their cell or make applications for visits or to see the governor or receive special food on religious grounds, or report sick etc. The other half were unlocked, and the same routine was repeated.

They then queued for breakfast, which was served on the ones of each wing, half a landing at that time. The serving areas being just below the central iron grill, breakfast being a full English or porridge, dished out and cooked by prisoners overseen by a kitchen chief and supervisory officers. Everything went smoothly, and on returning to their cells with their breakfasts were given a razor blade from a numbered pouch and again locked up and given any mail that had passed the censors. The whole routine was completed by eight fifteen, when the staff, myself included, went for breakfast in the officer's mess.

I sat with three of my mates, and we all ordered full English from the waiters, who were also prisoners, as were the chefs. My order came a few minutes after the others; the eggs were hard, the toast was burnt, and the sausages were undercooked. I could see that everyone in the mess was waiting for my reaction as the waiter flounced off with a grin.

"Hey, you, what's this mess"? I half shouted, not wanting to attract any more attention than was necessary but wanting to assert my authority.

"That's what you ordered, sir". The mess went deathly quiet and I could feel myself beginning to blush.

"I'm not having this muck; it's overcooked; change it immediately", my voice getting a little louder.

"I can't change it. The chef will be livid," he retorted in the most effeminate voice a twenty-two-year-old had ever heard.

"Listen, you puff, change it now" I knew after resorting to abuse, I'd lost this confrontation, but my humiliation was not complete.

"Have you ever tried it?" He asked in a voice tinged with triumph and a knowing nod of his head.

"No, I haven't, and I don't intend to" was my righteous response.

"Then don't knock it till you've tried it".

My face was becoming redder as the onlookers burst into raucous laughter.

I glanced at my mates, who were sniggering uncontrollably with the smuggest of looks.

I'd been well and truly set up and I fell in the trap but did eventually get my breakfast.

On returning to our respective landings and starting to unlock, we were told to lock up all inmates until further notice. We were then ordered to D1, a landing housing some of the nation's most notorious and violent prisoners. About thirty staff were already gathered, opposite a cell where an extremely angry man was stood in the doorway shouting and cursing and trying to get someone to confront him. He had tied a knife to his left hand with a part torn sheet with several razor blades were protruding above his knuckles. His upper torso was naked, he had slashed his body which was oozing blood and was covered in his own shit. He had a chair leg in his right hand.

Two officers stood opposite him with a mattress in front goading him out of his doorway. It took a few minutes, but he eventually stuck his head out beyond the brick abutments and was promptly whacked on the head by truncheons on either side.

The chief officer ordered me and Pete to take him in his half-dazed state to the hospital. Wrapping him in clean sheets and holding our noses, we led him along E wing to the hospital. Poor bastard had a dear John and had nowhere to go with his anger.

That was the start of my first full day. I wondered what else could happen and began to ponder my decision not to question my posting. Normal service resumed, the razor blades collected and inmates on cleaning duties were allowed out of their cells. Staff then manned the workshops and strategic points on route. When all was ready, the centre P.O. ordered unlock, and the cells were opened. The fours by two officers then dropped to the threes, and those unlocking the twos would then drop to the ones and unlock. The routine was so tested that everything ran smoothly. The rest of the day was uneventful, and as cleaning officer on A wing, I ensured that all the landings were clean and clear of any rubbish, it being the main thoroughfare to the officer's mess. A similar routine at the end of the prisoner's working day with the workshops being emptied and each prisoner is given a rub-down search. Surprisingly all were so used to the system it rarely faltered.

By five o'clock, all the workshops were empty of workers; they had collected their dinners and were locked away and ready to be counted. The staff would then gather at the centre, waiting for the count to be verified by the 'centre' P.O., if correct a stampede of officers would rush for the exit as if escaping their imprisonment.

My twelve-month probationary passed without any incidents, and I soon became an experienced officer. Seniority was not earned by experience or ability but by when you took up your post. Anyone joining Wandsworth after myself was deemed to be junior. I was considered to be competent for most duties. The 'ropes' were not difficult to learn, and the routines were so repetitive it would take an idiot to foul up. The variety of the judicial system was never-ending,

17

and I accepted the opportunity to take responsibility for the duties I was given.

CHAPTER 5
MY FIRST REPORT

On E1, the punishment landing was a special cell made into a court that administered justice to offenders of the prison rules. Whenever an officer reported an infringement, he was required to give his evidence to the judge (governor); the suspect was then given a chance to put his side of the story, and the governor then gave his verdict. Rarely giving deference to the prisoner, the punishment was swift and often harsh, loss of remission being the most feared judgment.

My written statement, handed to the Chief Officer the day before, was checked.

I then gave my verbal evidence

"Sir, date, time and place stated".

"I had no choice but to place them on report; confusion had caused a delay in the prison routine, resulting in the staff being late for their breakfast and the knock-on effect continuing until lunchtime."

"I saw this man (prison no) Jackson steal a sausage from (prison no) Wilson. Wilson took offence at this and struck Jackson in the face. Jackson retaliated and kicked Wilson. A fight ensued. It took myself and several members of staff to quell the situation and prevent the incident from spreading, onlookers becoming vocal and aggressive."

Jackson, wearing slippers, facing the governor, stood between two burly members of staff with their backs to the governor.

"Have you anything to say?" asked the governor.

"It's as the officer states, sir, except it was Wilson who stole my sausage first, and the officer only saw me trying to retrieve my sausage. I did hit Wilson and admit it got a bit out of hand".

"Thank you" replied the governor. "Seven days loss of earnings and privileges; dismissed". Jackson was then escorted to his cell.

Next up was Wilson, same routine and similar verbal evidence. Now, Wilson must have thought he had got away with it when he said, "Where is the evidence?"

"You mean, where is the sausage"? Asked the governor.

All eyes turned to me, and I was embarrassed to say that it was nowhere to be found and must have disintegrated during the fight.

Wilson was now gaining confidence and asked to be dismissed as there was no physical evidence to prove he stole a sausage.

"Seven days loss of earnings and privileges, dismissed.

He was then escorted to his cell.

That was the first time I had placed anyone on the report, and I was amazed at the speed of it. No long-drawn-out drama, swift justice and the correct punishment. No complaints.

Every time anyone was put on report, the governor administered justice in favour of his staff, and therefore, he had their respect and backing. There were occasions when this was taken advantage of by staff with dubious grounds for reporting minor incidents to get revenge on cons who bore threats and grudges.

The following events, as with the previous chapters, are all true and are the start of a succession of experiences. Recalled, as I remember them, not in any specific sequence of time or order, but close enough and contain my observations and insights as I witnessed them.

CHAPTER 6
BATH HOUSE DUTIES

Duties for the following day were put on the notice board giving the place of work such as Mailbags 1, Brush shop, Laundry, Censors, Reception, and Perimeter Patrol. These were all duties within the prison grounds and allocated by the duty P.O.

My duty this day was Bath House. I and another officer were to collect around forty filthy prisoners from Mailbags 1 and deliver them to the bath house. Every prisoner was to bathe once a week and entitled to clean clothes from the laundry. Water no more than nine inches deep and time allotted to be no longer than ten minutes. This was working o.k., as each batch finished another lot arrived, timing was essential, and any delay could create a backlog. "The water's not draining away", shouted one of the bathhouse cleaners.

Eighty baths not emptying would be a disaster. The outside drain is blocked and backing up inside. The cleaner tried clearing the drain by putting his hand down the outside gully. Senior officer O'Shaughnessy was beginning to panic; the repercussions could be enormous. The spread of disease may be rapid in such a close-knit community, and tempers could flare at the slightest provocation, representations to the governor and Board of Visitors about the lack of provision for personal hygiene. This problem could soon get out of hand, and so that's why he did what he did; he took matters into his own hand, thrusting it into the gulley as far as he could, emerging triumphantly with a huge solid turd claiming it was a short piece of pipe. Questions were asked among us as to why it hadn't disintegrated. No satisfactory conclusion was arrived at, except perhaps someone had chronic constipation. Stifled laughter from prisoners and staff as he realised what he was holding. The cleaner disappeared, but the day was saved, and the water flowed again.

The same evening, he was asked to check a cell on E2 where the spyglass had been broken, and something was blocking the viewing hole. O'Shaugnessy was a blustery type of character, and he used his whistle to push the obstruction away. He then put his face to the open spyglass as a dollop of shit was pushed into his eye. Stunted laughter surrounded him with comments such as "One in the eye for you, Jim" and "What a shitty day you're having, and your hand-eye coordination is working well". He lived down the embarrassment after a couple of weeks when someone else had an unfortunate episode of embarrassing humiliation.

CHAPTER 7
BEWARE YOUR THOUGHTS

I had a lot of respect for many prisoners, and one of them was an ex-boxer called O'Hanlon; he didn't seem to let anything bother him, and our respect, I think, was mutual. One morning on B1 I heard a lot of cheering just before breakfast, and it stopped almost as soon as it started. When I went to investigate, I saw three cons spark out on the floor, hardly moving. O'Hanlon stood nearby and showed me the Daily Mirror with the headline of a bomb going off and the I.R.A. claiming responsibility. The three guys on the floor were Irish. There were no complaints, and so I considered the matter dealt with satisfactorily.

The day-to-day running of the prison was mostly uneventful, with the occasional prisoner shouting abuse at an officer and being 'put on report' to maintain discipline. He would be escorted to E1 (chokey), the punishment landing and await trial the next morning. On a separate occasion, a few days later, I had a confrontation with O'Hanlon in front of prisoners, leaving me no choice but to place him on report.

"You've overstepped the mark in front of witnesses. You are nicked".

"No problem", he responded and went quietly to the chokey.

The next morning, in front of the Governor, standing between Hugh Jones and Jack Moore and

wearing slippers. He admitted the offence.

"Anything to say in your defence asked the governor

"Nothing to say"

"Seven days solitary."

O'Hanlon started to laugh, which did not impress the governor.

"I just had a thought," said O'Hanlon.

"Keep your thoughts to yourself", the governor responded.

"I can't get punished for thinking."?

"That's right".

"In that case, I think you're a cunt".

"Ten days Solitary, see what you think about that".

He served his ten days solitary, treating it like a holiday, no visits to the pub or the seaside. I assumed he gained some inner strength from solitude and used it to regain his personal discipline or to gain some notoriety of having breezed through his confinement. E1 was the punishment landing, where offending prisoners were placed in solitary confinement. They still had their rights, such as a bath once a week, one hour of exercise a day, three meals a day and visitation rights by family and friends. Privileges such as tobacco, working, and evening classes were curtailed for the length of their sentence. Usually a week to ten days unless a serious offence had been committed.

There is a slight trepidation when again coming face to face with someone who you put in solitary. Not so with O'Hanlon; he nodded and winked at me as if I had done him a favour, which I probably had, judging by his attitude as he emerged from E1 and went back to work.

CHAPTER 8
YARD PARTY

Not as it sounds, a barbecue, drinks, women and dancing but the opposite. With four prisoners, my duty for the day was to supervise the cleaning and collecting of rubbish thrown out of the windows or discarded during exercise. Mostly shit parcels in newspapers, shit in socks, sweet wrappers and any other rubbish. Several of the single cells on the C wing were being converted into units for four prisoners. As we reached the outside of C wing, I glanced up at the windows and saw a paper parcel being ejected. It sailed through the air and landed at my feet as I sidestepped. I was mad as hell as it burst open and sprayed my boots with shit. I clocked the cell window and counted from the recess windows to locate the exact cell, put the shit on a shovel and entered the wing from the side gate. I went directly up to the threes and counted back from the recess; it was a newly converted four-cell. The door was open, and three prisoners were eating their dinner at a table. It looked surprisingly civilised; I had left the yard party unsupervised and hesitated slightly before throwing the contents of the shovel on the floor whilst shouting that recess was the place for this crap.

"We're not animals", came an equally angry reply.

"One of you is!" I shouted back even louder.

As I left the cell and hurried back to my party, I realised that they had only just arrived with their lunch, and I could have misjudged the cell location. I was still mad but had a doubt that stayed with me the rest of the day.

They complained to the governor the next morning about my behaviour, even though one of them was wearing several bruises and a right shiner. Nothing else about it was mentioned.

CHAPTER 9
CELL SEARCH D WING

On some days, a thorough cell search of a landing suspected of carrying suspicious goods or drugs would be carried out. This involved all available staff, D1 was the suspected landing having new inhabitants who attempted to tunnel their way out of a recreation room in Parkhurst Prison on the Isle of Wight. Two of the ringleaders were transferred to Wandsworth. Troublemakers were always welcome. Me and Pete were given a cell and a prisoner to search. The con would bring out his bedroll and clothing, which I searched outside his cell. Pete went in and searched through his other items, tapping the walls with his truncheon, listening for any hollow sounds.

"Hey Pete, this guy tried to escape from Parkhurst, that's why he's here. Give it a good going over".

The prisoner seemed unruffled; no drugs or hollow sounds were found. However, a month later, I unlocked a cell on B3, and the same guy looked at me and started laughing. "You took ten years off my life when you searched my cell and told the other screw to be thorough. I nearly died; I had been removing bricks from behind my picture board". He had used porridge to replace the mortar, discarded when slopping out but was discovered by security a few days later. His laughter was so infectious it was impossible not to join in; his relief was obvious.

The P.O. in charge of the D wing was also the acting chief officer by the name of Hugill. A fair and even-handed officer of considerable experience with a wicked sense of humour. He was taking applications in his office.

"Next", called P.O. Hugill. "Name"? he asked.

"Ugle," said Ugle "Pronounced like bugle without the 'b', like your name".

"That's not Ugle. That's fucking Ugly".

"I would like to send a visiting order to my wife".

"I suppose she's a fucking Ugly as well".

"Well, yes, but a lot prettier than me.

It was all said with good humour and restraint. Ugle received his V. O., and Hugill shouted for the next in line.

Prisoner Jolly addressed the P.O., asking for directions to the exit; he did this most mornings, holding his bedroll and wearing a big smile while expecting to be released. Not today was the usual reply, which Jolly, without argument accepted. Turning on his heels he would return to his cell still wearing the smile he started the day with. He was of eastern origin which made me think he had some mystic knowledge that couldn't dampen his faith. His enthusiasm was infectious and lightened the mood of all who encountered him. When leaving his cell for meals he would do several somersaults along the landing with a benign, serene expression. He was a continually happy man no matter what happened.

CHAPTER 10
G.H.K. WINGS. PLUS

Wandsworth was built for almost seven hundred prisoners but had a population of over one thousand six hundred in 1969. Other parts not previously mentioned were G, H, and K wings which was a women's prison in its day. Four landings to a wing but no basement on K wing; used primarily for those who had been convicted but were awaiting sentence. G4 was for those placed under Rule 43, protection during their sentence and segregated from mainstream prison. Paedophiles (nonce) cases are those who grassed up someone or were avoiding some conflict or threats by others within the system.

"I unlocked on H2 this morning and couldn't believe my eyes; there was a woman with boobs and stuff", said Ted.

Had to check the record and she has had a sex change, or rather he has had a sex change. Not sure of what the crime was but was convicted and sent here. He/she is a rule fourteen three (awaiting medical reports) before sentencing. He/she had an operation and the judge was unsure whether to send him/her to Holloway (women's prison). The only logic he could arrive at was that he/she was born a man and verified by his/her birth certificate, so sent him/her to Wandsworth until the medical reports were submitted.

My whole perception of sexuality became blurred; there were men, and there were women. Some men were homosexual, and some women were Lesbian, simple and unblurred categories of sexuality. Clearly understood and not too complicated, then you come up with more

30

dilemmas such as bisexual and transexual, bewildering and complicating.

Chatting with Ted, Pete and Dave in the officer's mess at morning break we discussed the best way of handling the situation, if ever any strange happenings should occur. We couldn't arrive at likely scenarios, but we did notice Geoff Jackson sitting at the next table prick up his ears at the mention of the word sex. Ted tilting his head in his direction and in a stage whisper said.

"He's heterosexual, you know".

"Not me," said Geoff indignantly. "I'm not a bleeding heterosexual".

"We think you are" responded Pete with sympathy.

"Don't you start spreading lies about me", retorted Geoff with much assertion.

"We were always a little suspicious about you Geoff".

He became increasingly enraged, which encouraged Dave to say.

"He who protesteth too much"!!

"Don't you quote Dickens to me; I'll report you to the governor for spreading malicious lies."

"I've met his wife, and she is in amateur dramatics and that makes her a thespian".

"Listen, you lot, just one more word, and you are dead", he shrieked.

"A man's gotta do what a man's gotta do", smiled Pete.

"That was a cruel wind up", as we fell about laughing at the best wind up for a long time. A wicked sense of humour is essential to alleviate the boredom.

CHAPTER 11
ESCORT DUTIES

Any duty to get away from the nick was always welcome. My first as a junior officer was to Marylebone Magistrates court, handcuffed to a prisoner appearing as a witness for the defence. My role was to stick as close as possible to him when giving his evidence from the witness box. He was locked in the cells awaiting his turn which gave me a chance to find the loos (had a few beers the night before). I was told to be careful about choosing the right door to have a pee. I was alarmed and confused at what I saw when I opened what I thought was the right door. Two rows of police sat on benches staring at each with more firepower than the Magnificent Seven. I almost asked for the urinals but thought better of it as I realised, I'd chosen the wrong door. When the witness was called to give his evidence, I was given a chair to sit on behind the witness box while he was cross-examined. There was a lull in proceedings when everything seemed suspended in time, all eyes were on the witness as he faltered in his speech. Suddenly the loudest fart south of Watford Gap reverberated around the court, not a word was said, just a visual sign of flared nostrils and a look of disdain toward the witness from the onlookers. Of course I was innocent of such a sordid sound and shrugged my shoulders in disapproval in the direction of the witness. I did get many escort duties during my time at Wandsworth and will recount some more throughout the rest of this book.

CHAPTER 12
ST. GEORGES HOSPITAL GUARD

Guarding a prisoner who was too ill to be in the prison hospital was a good number. Just myself dressed in civvies guarding a prisoner called Richardson who had suffered a broken neck while previously attempting to escape. I was fortunate to be on the three until eleven shift, which meant I saw all the activity and routines of the hospital staff and visitors.

Richardson, a Category A prisoner was to be guarded with caution and treated as a normal patient with the visiting rights and procedures of anyone else on the ward. Food, pyjamas and as many visitors as allowed during the times stated by the hospital. His neck was in constant traction, making it difficult to eat and drink; a band round his forehead attached to a wire with a specific weight keeping his head still for most of the day and night meant it was unlikely he would escape. That was the summation all his guards made. I was sat in a chair adjacent to his bed reading Catch Twenty-Two, a brilliant read I couldn't put down. Les Britton relieved me at eleven o'clock, and I went home. My hospital duty finished two days later, and I was given night duty at the prison.

At about two o'clock, a call from the hospital went something like this. He's not here, sir, and I can't find him anywhere; I've searched the whole ward and the loos, and I cannot find him. His pyjamas are here and his slippers, but not Richardson. What shall I do? I only went to the loo for a couple of minutes. Ulcer Yates took the call and replied, screaming in panic, "Hang your fucking keys up". The ulcer of Yates that night became more inflamed than ever. Richardson was recaptured a couple of weeks later; it came to light that he'd been exercising during the times when his guards were absent for whatever reason. His visitors had brought him clothes and money to aid in his escape. The fact he was on the third floor made it seem less likely that he could abscond down a drainpipe. Les didn't lose his job but was forever threatening to leave.

CHAPTER 13
WEEKEND WORKING

The V scheme was a system of working all the duties required. It would work well if there was enough staff., but because of the shortage, a day of rest was once every fourteen days. Although the workshops were closed, the prison still had its routine. Inmates were still fed, applications were still made, and prison visits made the weekends really busy. Tension was always a little more fraught when spare time was boring, radios were not yet allowed, and the only exercise inmates were entitled to was for one hour walking on a purpose-built paved Circle. Category A prisoners were notorious criminals who would cause embarrassment to the Home Office if they escaped and to the prison authorities. Each Cat A was not allowed to mix with other prisoners. Wherever they were allowed to go they had a passbook which was handed over to the next officer who signed, timed and placed the log.

Their visits were conducted in the main entrance corridor toward the Centre. A maximum of two visits at a time were allowed. The Cat A con would enter through a glazed door into a room divided by a half-glazed partition and escorted by a screw who signed his passbook. The visitors would then come in through another glazed door into the other half of the divided room escorted by a screw and sit in a cubicle opposite the Cat A and have half hours visit. When time was up the prisoner was escorted back to his cell and the visitors escorted to the gate. Time was limited and strict if a lot of visitors were expected.

I told one prisoner his time was up and to vacate his seat as the next visit was due to commence. He totally ignored my request and carried on talking to his wife and kids. I gave him a couple more minutes before repeating my instruction. I repeated myself twice more and warned him of the consequences. He turned round and told me to fuck off.

The alarm systems in most prisons were three pushes on the button for non-urgent situations, but send two officers when numbers allow. Two pushes means not drastic but send four officers ASAP. The alarm system in Wandsworth did not register two or three pushes, if the button was pushed the cavalry arrived. There was no communication system in the visiting room, only an alarm bell, no radio or phone. Two prisoners on my side of the room and an alarm bell. Four adults and two kids on the other side of the divide and one officer. I had no choice but to push the button.

In no time at all about fifty screws appeared, I pointed to the prisoner, who he was hauled away cursing and screaming. His wife and kids were witnesses to this act of restraint. It was reported on the news that night what had happened, but with a bias slant.

Sunday was a more relaxed day with visitors being civil and the visited amiable. Church may have had something to do with it as the Bishop of Streatham was giving the service in the chapel above the main entrance. It could hold a goodly and godly number of parishioners. The bishop greeted everyone warmly, some kissed his ring, others bowed and others peered curiously. The service was well attended and enjoyable with the hymns sang with gusto and intent. Onward Christian Soldiers being the final hymn.

Well, I've never heard a hymn sang with such clarity and inspiring purpose as on that day. It with a fairly standard quiet tempo, building steadily with a rising chorus. Sung beautifully and energetically performed with swelling pride. Come the final verse I was so taken aback just had to join in, it was a joy to be a part of and just before the final chorus someone shouted 'One More Time'. I didn't think this could be bettered but it was belted out even louder and the crescendo was deafening. "God heard us today", smiled one prisoner on leaving.

CHAPTER 14

EVENING DUTY

Evening duty was in addition to a normal day's work and would finish at eight forty-five when the night staff arrived. A reduced number of officers allocated to each wing would unlock 'students' enrolled on evening classes. Most subjects were covered Maths, English, History etc. and other religions. Knitting, needlework and crocheting were not on the curriculum but may have been oversubscribed if allowed.

Classes lasted an hour and tutors who were vigorously vetted would give lessons in various rooms close to the centre. After lessons were over students returned to their cells and 'cocoa' patrol would commence. All prisoners were given a balanced diet three times a day, and anyone on special diets for health reasons or religious or being vegetarians or vegans were catered for by the kitchen.

'Cocoa' patrol gave every prisoner irrespective of their diet a mug of tea and a cake about an hour before lights out. Two screws and five prisoners from each wing would collect from the kitchen two large urns of tea and a massive tray of cake. Starting on the fours as the first cell was unlocked by the officer in front eager hands grabbed the cake and mugs held out for tea. No more than four cells at a time were unlocked, and as each one received his supper.

Endearments such as have a good night's sleep, don't let the bedbugs bite, see you in the morning light were imparted. Lullabies were frowned upon and songs such as Goodnight Sweetheart were banned.

It would take just over an hour to do the cocoa run and supplies would be renewed as needed. When finished and the count was verified staff would often gather in groups of three or four on the iron floor grill nearest the exit and generally, chat about the day and what duty they were assigned for the next day.

Officers' hats of standard issue had a flat peak similar to a baseball cap but shiny and quite straight. The slashing of peaks was frowned upon, but even so a lot had been altered in order to appear tough and look authoritative and from a military background. Pigeons rarely created a problem, their droppings normally dodged by alert staff, except on one occasion when Keith Gray who talked a lot but said nothing of note recounted a story of the time he was court officer at the Old Bailey during a very harrowing rape trial. The woman who'd been raped was unable to say to the court the precise words the rapist used when he had finished with her. Her embarrassment and sense of shame on view to the gallery and the court officials.

The judge intervened and asked her to write down what was said so it could be produced as evidence. This she did with great reluctance and handed the note to the court usher who then went to give it to the clerk of the court who was sitting beneath the judge. Unfortunately the clerk had dozed off which was noticed by the judge who impatiently took the note from the usher. The judge after reading the contents leaned over from his raised position, shook the clerk and handed him the note. Whereupon the clerk on waking read the note, looked at the judge in dismay, and with the look of a told off schoolboy left the court.

Just as he finished the story a dropping fell from the roof and hit a non-slashed peak hat which directed the pigeon waste into the mouth of the non-slashed peak, which happened to be the storyteller. From pigeon shit to bullshit with a judicial twist. The pigeons were the only free birds doing bird at Wandsworth. They were mostly grey, prisoners were grey, their uniforms were grey, the walls were grey, the flagstones were grey, the wire fence was grey, the internal road was grey, cell doors were grey and Keith was Gray and full of shit. After the night shift arrived and took over at eight forty-five the evening staff would go home or to the County Arms.

CHAPTER 15
NIGHT DUTY

Wandsworth by day can be a scary place, but at night it had an eerie sense of restrained fear. Being locked in a cell is terrifying and I was locked in for an hour once when I forgot to, ' shoot the bolt' got pushed in and the door shut behind me. I was there an hour and my ringing of the cell bell brought no rescue. The rising panic and dread that I might be forgotten was overwhelming. That's what was in those cells at night, a hundred years of heavy, creepy unease, it permeated the walls creeping into the atmosphere and breathed into the psyche of all left on duty. The sense of humour being heightened to disguise the unease.

Five night staff in the main prison, one to each wing, two in G.H.K. wings, two to the hospital, three to patrol the inner road, plus one dog patrol and two at the main gate. A P.O. would be the man in charge, and the only person with any keys. One man to a wing would check the count as he switched the lights off each cell in turn also looking for any attempted suicides. Once completed and the count checked four of us would settle down to play cards A half hour pegging system was used to ensure that each wing was patrolled, each peg strategically placed and time logged in the office once pressed. Random checks on cells throughout the night were often done if suspicious noises were heard.

I thought I heard a noise from this cell on E4 so I checked through the spyglass after turning on the light and couldn't see a thing, I called the P.O. and he hurriedly unlocked the door. Three of us pushed really hard to open the door to find a man sliding to the floor, a wire coat hanger cutting into his neck had been suspended from the top edge. Oozing blood, lips turned blue and his bulging eyes and limp body told us he was dead. Opening the door released the pressure on the hanger and he slumped to the floor.

"Give him the kiss of life" yelled Ulcer Yates as he radioed the hospital.

"He's dead", replied a stunned looking Dave.

"Not until a doctor confirms it, we have to try and resuscitate him".

Looking at each other we attempted chest presses in turn until the doctor arrived and confirmed what we already knew.

E wing was nearest to the prison hospital where anyone serving over five years was placed, their behaviour assessed for a month until transferred to the main prison, usually E wing. The night then wore on slowly and the card games ended as a morose air of finality hit us all.

A different duty each night made it interesting. I was given a duty in the hospital where I was locked in a square ward behind an iron gate. The 'patients' were an unknown quantity in regard to their crimes and some only arrived from court that day. I was a qualified first aider and that was all, how could I cope with a murderer or any malicious thug who had nothing to lose but take vengeance out on the first uniform he sees, me. He could be psychotic, schizophrenic or a plain old nasty bastard.

Locked in at nine o'clock and not relieved until seven was a long time to stay awake. The only access to a loo was the other side of the ward and out of reach of the alarm bell (no cavalry on night duty). All I had to do was to sit at a desk close to the gate, and press a button every fifteen minutes and make sure the patients were up, dressed and ready for breakfast at seven a.m.

I did not go to the loo or move from my station all night, did not eat or drink just to be on the safe side. At six thirty I roused the inmates to get dressed 'rise and shine' I called at six thirty with as much assertion as I could muster. A few surly and old-fashioned glances came my way which I ignored with disdain. Seven a.m. and the hospital staff arrived, I was abundantly pleased to be relieved and I walked home in double quick time.

G.H.K. wings at one time was a women's prison, now being used for remands, those convicted but not yet sentenced and awaiting psychiatric reports (section 14/3) and probationary reports (section29). Court protocol was that each convicted man attend court for sentencing every fourteen days whether the judge had made a decision or not. This must have been very costly, as sentencing in extreme circumstances could take months.

The next night me and Ted were on night patrol in G.H.and k wings. The wings were smaller than the main prison so only two screws needed. The clocking pegs were located at the farthest points from the centre. The office was out of bounds, but there was a room where we could chat and while away the night between pegging every half hour.

One would sleep for half the night while the other did the pegging and then we'd swap to share the duty.

There was a cell on H 4 at the far end that was never occupied, dirty white tiles on the walls, floor never cleaned and the door never locked. The story was that a woman was killed in there whilst having a shower. That her ghost haunted the cell; the door left ajar in the hope she would leave. During the day it had a presence that sent a shiver down the back of the neck of the most sceptical of us. Next to that cell was one of the pegs of course. A storm brewing that night and when it was my turn to do the rounds, the moon was full, the wind howling through the broken pains of the large glass window next to the cell and Ted was asleep in the night patrol room.

Now I'm not a believer in the supernatural, but when I came to press that peg the recesses on that wing all flushed at the same time, sending the pigeons flying. Lightening momentarily lit up the whole wing as the wind blasted through the broken panes; a groan and a creak as the door opened a little more, behind which I saw a grey shape appearing to float just beneath the barred window. My heart skipped a beat as the rear of my trousers flapped a little. I hurriedly fled that landing and went to the next pegging point telling myself it was my overactive imagination and tiredness playing tricks on me.

When I reached the rest room on G 2 Ted was still asleep, or was he? I had my doubts but didn't want to give him the satisfaction that his prank worked. I would surely have heard his footsteps, unless he was wearing his socks. He would have been really quick to get back when

I pegged K 3. He could have dropped to the two's whilst I ran along the three's and got to the rest room before I noticed. It played on my mind for the rest of the night and when it was my turn to sleep, I couldn't. I rationalised it as the weather, the pigeons the recesses, the moon the groaning and the sighting as a rare coincidence. Never spoke of it to Ted and he didn't either.

The next night I was patrolling the internal road that ran between the external wall and the fence. Dog handlers also patrolled the same road, it being U shaped with a patrol box at each corner meant we could always see the other patrolling officer. Part of the first section was close to reception, which was also next to an historical graveyard, no headstones or crosses visible.

Now I'm not a believer in ghosts or spirits, but after the experience of the previous night I just couldn't bring myself to walk anywhere near that part of the prison. I wasn't afraid or scared in any way, it's just that my legs had a mind of their own and refused to patrol that area. Night duty was for seven nights with no two duties being repeated. So why was I given the hospital again? My objections were dismissed, and I considered going off sick, but my pride was marginally stronger than my fear.

A second night locked in with prisoners at the start of their minimum five-year sentences, not knowing who or what they were in for. I relaxed a little with my feet on the desk, pegging every fifteen minutes and trying not to fall asleep. When in a state of deep relaxation, I fell off my chair at the sound of the loudest scream of obscenities from someone three beds away. He was sat bolt upright in his bed unaware he had woken everyone in the ward. You pratt Prosser came the angry response from the adjacent bed when he just as quickly returned to his sleeping position totally unaware of what had happened. We were all awake except Prosser until the day staff arrived.

The next night we arrived at eight forty-five, me Ted, Dave, Pete and Gerry were all on duty in the main prison, which meant we could play cards to pass the time. But first we took our packed meals and flasks of tea to the rest room on E 2, which happened to be the 'Topping Shed'. Maintained and ready for use if needed. There were still offences where a hanging could be carried out, for example arson in Her Majesty's dockyard or treason. This was used as a night patrol rest room and a snacking place or for a quick kip.

The evening staff just left as we prepared for the night when a message came over the walkie talkie that an officer had been shot outside the main gate. Disbelief, incredulity and 'this is a wind up' was an automatic response followed by 'it could have been me' relief when the incident was confirmed a couple of minutes later. Cliff Endersby a Senior Officer finished his evening duty and was on his way home to his wife and kids when a van drove up beside him and a shotgun blast hit him in the back of the legs. Stunned and helpless, unable to respond to help a colleague, locked inside frustrated and angry the atmosphere was instantly changed from routine to us and them. Speculation as to why was left for the investigating team and the police.

Although the whole truth I felt was never revealed it seemed that the reason for the shooting was because an I.R.A. prisoner residing on D wing had been put on report for verbally abusing an officer that day. Whilst being escorted to E1, the punishment landing, he tripped on the stone steps and hurt his pride. Bad news travels fast inside, and even faster to the outside, repercussions could have enormous implications for staff and their families. Fortunately, there were no more incidents related to that occurrence although as a footnote the deputy governor was seen perched in a tree outside the entrance for several days, there were no leaves on the trees therefore he was visible to everyone especially the general public, which I think was his intention for which he was we applauded.

The night routine carried on, lights turned out and the count confirmed. D wing was Patrolled more often than usual with the stamping of boots and the odd clanging of truncheon on railing.

CHAPTER 16
ESCORT TO PARKHURST

A coachload of prisoners were often sent to prisons on the Isle of Wight, Camp Hill, Albany and Parkhurst almost every Wednesday. The coach was a large Pixie which could hold fifty or more on a trip to the seaside and a ride on a ferry. This day Wednesday 23 May 1973 was eventful. O'Hanlon the boxer was on board as well as eighteen other detainees and the required number of officers. The trip to the ferry was uneventful until we reached and boarded the boat. Some prisoners became a little agitated and started pointing at a group of men at the bow of the ferry boat. The senior officer alerted us all to be extra vigilant and be ready to draw truncheons if necessary. Ted asked to leave the coach to use the loo on board; on leaving he calmly walked up to the group of men in question and began chatting to them, anxious looks following him from staff and prisoners alike. He then waved to the coach and pointed to the guys next to him giving a thumbs up signal. A mixed signal until one of us noticed it was members of Monty Pythons Flying Circus taking in the sea air, sighs of relief all round, and a few autographs signed.

The Daily Mirror that morning led with a front-page story about a known villain, 'George Ince Not Guilty' was the headline. He had been on trial accused of murdering Muriel Patience, of shooting her husband, and daughter, but this day was the day of the retrial and his acquittal. New evidence had been submitted giving him an alibi. He had previously been reluctant to give the name of Dolly Grey who he was with on the day of the murder. Anyone who followed the case knew this was Dolly Kray wife of Charlie Kray and elder brother of the Kray twins; including O'Hanlon.

After arriving at Parkhurst and handing over the prisoners to reception staff I recognised the Kray twins. They had some authority and control of movement within Parkhurst. They processed the intake and as O'Hanlon passed through their hands he remarked,

"I see Charlie's wife was being shagged by Ince". No response from the Krays, a slight glance up was all they did, but an ominous sense of foreboding dramatically changed the atmosphere.

Although reception was ultimately controlled by staff, the influence and input by sadistic and violent thugs may have been a shrewd move by the management. Carrying on to Albany and Camp hill to deposit the rest of the prisoners was light relief and welcomed by all.

Returning to Wandsworth with a few transferees who were left at reception we decided to have a cuppa in the mess. Dave was in there and asked how the trip went,

"News arrived an hour ago, that O'Hanlon had been attacked, the muscles in his upper arms had been severed and his eye lids cut off."

When I got home and watched the evening news, there was Lord Longford advocating on behalf of the Krays. Despite an incident today in which they were involved at Parkhurst he strongly recommended they be considered for early parole.

I could never discuss my work with my wife, thinking it too brutal and disturbing for a woman to hear.

CHAPTER 17
FARM PARTY

This was reputed to be a cushy number, take four trusted prisoners (red bands) in a pixie to the grounds of the headquarters of the fire service in Dorking. A mansion with all the trimmings, tennis court, trout stream, pheasant and beautiful gardens. After asking several previous supervisors for advice on what the duties were, I was informed that there was no specific routine and that the red bands knew what was required. As the pixie pulled up just inside gate and the door slid back; I was about to get out when all four of them scarpered.

I was left with the distinct feeling that they were up to something. I hadn't a clue where they were and resisted an impulse to blow my whistle which would have brought them back immediately to my custody. I wandered around for at least ten minutes in a state of bewilderment calling out to them like a father calls for his children, tentatively with repressed anger.

"Over here gov", called a disembodied voice from amongst the rhododendrons. I followed the voice which raised my sense of smell. Bacon was frying somewhere as the aroma of coffee wafted by my nose. Familiar smells eased my anxiety a little as I saw a very smart garden shed. Inside was luxury, one red band was cooking a full English breakfast, five chairs surrounding a table clothed in gingham. Cutlery, plates, mugs and napkins were placed at each chair and even a vase of flowers as a centre piece.

I was so relieved to see my farm party all together but had a suspicion that something happened in that ten minutes and that the seduction of breakfast was to deter any compulsion I may have to ask questions.

"I'll get you a pheasant", said one trustee. "They land in the fenced tennis court and are unable to fly out because the angle is too steep." Two were seen an hour later. "They're trapped", he whispered. As he entered the enclosure both birds flew over the fencing and escaped with feet to spare. "I'll get you a trout, from the stream, they can't fly."

The rest of the day was great, lawns cut, borders weeded, paths cleaned and a touch of sunbathing as an extra perk. Picked up at three thirty and back to the nick. I was lucky the Chief didn't arrive to inspect the grounds as on a previous visit he caught a shirtless officer fishing the stream with a garden cane and a thin piece of string tied to the bent tine of a kitchen fork. Arriving back at the nick 'Burglar' searched the red bands at the gate before entering the main prison, 'Burglars being two security staff with powers to search anyone at any time. Searching the Farm Party was standard procedure, having been outside the prison.

CHAPTER 18
RULE 43

G4 was where the sex case prisoners resided, placed there by the governor or at their own request to avoid being at large in the main prison, Rule 43 was their new identity. The worst sex offenders and notorious high-profile inmates the public could imagine. I had a look at the records of two of them and was so shocked and horrified that I promised myself not to look at anyone's record again, not because my stomach would retch at the findings or that my sensibilities would be challenged. But because my ability to do the job properly would be greatly impaired and influenced by my judgement of the subservient manner and cowering demeanour of such terrified individuals. My job was to make sure they were not attacked or harmed whilst under my wing as it were.

I rarely had sight of the governor, but he sought me out to ask me to allow two men to visit a particular rule 43 inmate. There was no record to be made as they were not seen entering the prison and will not be recorded leaving, therefore it never happened. I could have refused this cloak and dagger stuff, but I complied as long as I was within sight of the prisoner whilst he was interviewed and that the cell door was left ajar. I escorted the two men to the cell of the prisoner, unlocked the door, shot the bolt and told the inmate he had visitors. He went immediately white, and his body seemed to lose its structure. I told him that this was not an official visit and that he could refuse to talk to them. His fear of not talking to them was far greater than his fear of refusing their questions. I went to the other side of the landing where I could observe the proceedings through the open door. I was in a very precarious position myself if anything happened to him.

The interview lasted about half an hour and as they left his cell a nod in my direction signalled they were finished. The governor appeared from the central office and escorted the phantoms to the main gate. I was relieved to see that no physical harm had happened. I asked him what all the fuss was about. Noting he was extremely nervous and edgy I did not press him for an answer but strongly sensed he was desperate to unload. He gave some token resistance before he decided to spill the beans. He said that a flat in Chelsea had been burgled and some incriminating photographs had been stolen and could lead to a major embarrassment for a wealthy and well-respected London family. He did not want to explain any further as the visitors had calmly threatened to 'place him on the missing list'. I was astounded, sceptical and dumbfounded at these revelations but I believed him totally. I had many more questions myself but felt that the more I knew the more embroiled I would become and that discretion in this case was better than valour.

Rule 43 prisoners were kept separate from the main population, working and exercising as a group.

CHAPTER 19
A RARE NIGHT OUT

It was rare to have a night out with your mates, especially on a Friday evening and we made a decision to visit the Vauxhall Tavern. It was Geordies' (ex-matelot) idea and we all fell in line with it, the tavern having a reputation for being different. What an eye opener for a twenty-three year who had led a sheltered life. The place was heaving, the bar shaped like a snake, the staff wearing hotpants and braces and looking sweaty trying to cope with the throng of bodies thirsting for a drink. It was a very warm summer evening and getting to the bar needed patience, which was not a virtue where we were concerned. So we cut a single file and shouldered our way forward. Graham being the tallest and most noticeable managed to order a round.

"I know you, you bastard you work at the nick", said a thick set guy with a couple of mates.

"I know you as well", replied Graham as he passed the beer along "You were doing time"

"And I know him", he said aggressively as he saw Ted, who was taking the first pint from Graham.

"Stand aside" responded Ted "we are trying to get a drink".

"I know you as well" when he saw me taking the pint from Ted.

His aggression diminishing each time he saw a pint being passed along the line, and when the last pint reached Geordie, the round had been paid for by our new found friends, which was very nice of them.

Managing to gather in a group near the open window where conversation was reduced to a roar I began to look around. I was surprised to see attractive women with moustaches, facial hair. Males wearing women's clothes and others that were difficult classify to any recognisable gender. Gay was a word meaning happy or cheerful (unless you were a hussar) but now used to classify homosexuality.

"I will never be happy or cheerful, people will think I'm gay" said Graham as he backed up to the open window. Geordie the ex matelot had gone outside and as Graham said the word gay he grabbed his arse. The word gay has never been emitted with such a shrill and fearful outburst as that evening. It was so loud and 'gay' that Graham became the centre of unwelcome attention for the rest of the night, his face becoming redder giving the impression that he was being coy.

Cabaret was the film of the moment, and the bar was bedecked with 'Liza Minnelli's' sing to Mein Herr. Some were men, some were women, and some were something else. After drinking two pints I needed the loo, nervous about going on my own I asked if anyone else wanted to go, not the thing to ask in a gay pub. No response, so I squeezed my way past the revellers to what looked like a timber shed just off the centre of the lounge. Three troughs were occupied so I went to the fourth. My anxiety so apparent that my neighbour peered over the porcelain wing and looked at my manhood. His gaze followed my torso up to my fearful face and giving me a terrifying smile, he said "I could munch you" I told him to "Piss off "which backfired as I couldn't piss after that. I waited until all the troughs became vacant and I could piss in peace.

I told the lads; a bad mistake, for the next few weeks I was called Munchy the peaceful Pisser. Took a while to live it down Graham got called The Gay Boy, so I had some company. That was my first and last exposure to gay exhibitionism.

CHAPTER 20
JUST ANOTHER WARM DAY

After breakfast on a midweek day, another cell search was ordered on B3, and all available staff searched the entire landing. Mostly they were three to a cell which were built for one, my search mate stayed outside and rummaged through the bedrolls and belongings of each prisoner. I was unfortunately searching inside the cell and looking for anything suspicious, drugs, tobacco, knives or other weapons. I found a cardboard box about a foot square and a foot deep under the bunk. Picking up a pair of socks from the top and searching through the rest of the box I began to feel sick. The smell was familiar as I realised the socks were full of shit. With disgust and anger, I shouted "you dirty bastards are nicked" which echoed round the wing. My fury startled all concerned, myself included as I looked each one in the eye and as quickly as my outburst started it began to diminish. Realising that three in a cell was not the ideal accommodation for privacy and toilet discipline was not always possible. After telling them what I had found I left it to them to sort it out, besides I didn't have an appetite for producing a shitty pair of socks as evidence to the governor.

My next duty was to unlock one side of C3 and make sure each cell was empty as the inmates went to work. Hi Ho, Hi Ho was sometimes chanted as I checked and locked each cell on my way back. My colleague did the same on the other side of the landing when I heard an angry argument between him and a prisoner who was 'declining' go to work. The exchange became much more heated the longer it went on; I crossed the landing to give assistance. The inmate began to threaten us and was adamant that he was not going to work. I lost it and belted him a couple of times, placed him on report for assault and refusing to work. He can stay in his cell now as I locked the door.

My next duty was the Induction shop where recently convicted inmates were encouraged to sew mailbags to earn credits to buy stuff in the prison shop, such as tobacco, toothpaste, daily paper or other luxury items. I elected to sit in 'The Chair', a raised platform with an alarm and a panoramic view of the complete workshop. Giving the observer the power to decide who could go to the loo next. As soon as one of the cubicles became vacant a dozen hands would be thrust into the air requesting to be next. Smoking not allowed on the shop floor was overlooked when using the toilets. There was a face in the centre of the shop that was staring at me intently. I ignored this face, but whenever I had to decide who could be next to have a smoke and scanned the rows this face would still be staring at me. After half an hour I decide to glare back. As if in a battle to see who would blink, I controlled the shop using my peripheral vision, giving permission as I saw fit. At the finish of work for lunch I dismissed each row of inmates whilst still glaring at this face. My colleague giving each prisoner a rub down search as they left. Without taking my eyes off him I dismissed the row he was on and told him to stay put. The shop was now empty except for me and this face.

"Come here" I ordered pointing to the bottom of the steps leading to 'The Chair'. This he did without either one of us blinking. "What's your name" I asked with a trace of venom and when he responded with a smirk, I calmy walked down the steps and looked up at him as

60

he seemed to get taller with each step. Not taking my eyes off him I suddenly went to hit him in the stomach. He protected himself and I caught his wrist, if you hit anyone you expect to be hit back, but all he did was cower and whinge. This was a day I was taking no shit from anyone but I did expect a blow to be returned. I gave him a rub down search and sent him on his way.

It was 5.15 and I was the only officer to be seen on C3 with about eighty prisoners socialising with about five minutes before lock up. I began checking each cell as I banged them up when I came across this big guy in the wrong cell. Telling him to get a move on and get to his own cell was met with verbal abuse. He resisted my instruction and slammed the door shut. I put him on report and left him in the cell with his three mates. Expecting to go home after an eventful day was put back by five hours. Prisoners on D wing exercise yard formed a summer protest and decided to sit down and refused to move. All available staff were asked to observe the situation whilst senior staff decided what would be the best course of action.

The day staff of about sixty gathered at one end of the yard drinking tea and chatting as if it was a normal thing to happen and compared it to when this last occurred several years earlier. With raised voices they described how it transpired that the governor politely asked the squatters to retire to their cells and that there would be no punishment if they obeyed within ten minutes. A vociferous reply, coupled with jeering and derision was immediately responded to with a shrill blow on a whistle signalling the charge of a hundred extra officers hidden behind the end of D wing. The protestors were clambering over themselves to escape and return to their cells. That was the good old days remarked one old screw.

This protest was a little different in that they were more determined and felt this action was justified. The evening wore on and as the sun disappeared their resolve weakened with the lack of food, drink and the oncoming chill. The officer in charge gave them an ultimatum and a promise to listen to their grievances in the morning if they returned to their cells immediately; otherwise he would have the staff physically remove them from the yard. Slowly extra staff could be seen entering the yard, truncheons raised and looking for any excuse to get stuck in. As they clambered for the entrance they were halted and each prisoner was escorted by two discipline officers to their respective cells. On entering D wing there was several staff lining each landing, giving a show of force and a reminder of the need to follow the rules.

I got home after eleven that night exhausted and relieved that discipline had been maintained by Discipline Officers. Their grievances were listened to the next day and some were allowed but most needed to be relayed to the home office for them to consider. I had two on report for separate incidents and the first one coming in front of the governor apologised straight away without any evidence being given. He was due to be released the following day and had become overly excited at the thought of becoming a free man.

"Seven days loss of earnings and seven days in solitary", was the governors response. His release was delayed for a week. The next one up also apologised unreservedly to myself and accepted any punishment that was due. He was given seven days loss of privileges. On my way down E2 I almost bumped into 'The Smirker' on his way back from the hospital with his wrist in bandages. Dismayed I asked him what had happened and hurriedly and silently he carried on his way. I then bumped into the Chief officer who informed me there had been a complaint of assault made against me. He then continued that this complaint was not recorded officially and therefore was regarded as informative and no action was necessary.

Often there were long periods of boring routine, interspersed with the occasional outburst and ill-discipline from staff or inmates. Workshop supervision was without doubt the most tedious duty to be assigned. Usually two officers to a workshop plus a couple of trade staff overseeing up to a hundred and fifty cons, either sewing mailbags, making brushes or doing the laundry.

The prisoner's kitchen had their own staff of qualified officers supervising the running of perhaps the most important job inside the prison. The feeding of the inmates; providing nourishment through a balanced diet to every religion under the sun plus vegan, vegetarian and those with health issues requiring specialist foods. A logistical nightmare warranting the rank of Chief Officer down to discipline officer / kitchen, with Senior and Principal officers in between.

One such officer was nicknamed Hambone, a title he found very difficult to live down. During his probationary period he was given the responsibility one day to guard a huge bone of ham for a period of about two hours. Make sure that no one thieves it, that's all you have to do, was the order. It was never solved how the meat left the bone whilst under his vigilance, he did not leave his post or become distracted, so he said. Hence the nickname HamBone.

The staff in the hospital ranked from discipline officer up to Chief Officer with qualifications relevant to their duties. Anyone serving over five years was supervised in hospital for a month to assess their 'suitability' before entering the main prison. The administration block was run by civilians up to CEO level and held the records of staff and prisoners. The whole system was likened to a small village, almost self-sufficient, backed by a government who had a controlling interest and a responsibility to protect the public and to instil justice with an even hand and compassion.

CHAPTER 21
Other Escorts

When escorting high profile prisoners to the Old Bailey involved in serious crime that may take weeks to come to some conclusion, each prisoner was handcuffed to an officer and often driven by car, sometimes with police outriders in support and sometimes with decoy driven vehicles. The handcuffs were very heavy and shaped more like a large padlock with adjustable wrist sizes and linked with a substantial chain Houdini couldn't escape from.

My being a junior I was handcuffed to a prisoner who was being tried at Wimbledon Magistrates court where several other prisoners were charged with the same crime. A ring of armed police was clearly visible as we approached the court. There were six prisoners in the dock and each one was handcuffed to an officer which filled two benches. They had no respect for the court and derided a lady witness giving evidence. The court inspector was a little late arriving and crept in hoping not to be noticed. Tip Toe Through The Tulips became the song of the moment sung by the prisoners. The magistrate asked us to keep them quiet, which was like asking the impossible.

The next witness was Britain's first supergrass and as he arrived at the witness box a hum, barely audible at first, resonated from the two benches. It grew slowly and became more chilling as the words could be recognised. A rendition of Peggy Lees' 'We'll Meet Again' hung in the air, halting the proceedings. It didn't get any louder but maintained an even monotone with a disturbing certainty that there was no escape.

The witness was clearly unsettled as was I and a few others, my response to them to keep quiet and show respect was feeble and weakened by the realisation that they were so sure of revenge. Like all things that became unsettling, they were brushed off with a humour that disguised the fear.

Lancaster Prison was a castle and I was in charge with a junior officer handcuffed to a prisoner being transferred there. An overnight stay with subsistence and a visit to my relatives in Bolton-Le Sands; sometimes good luck did happen. I was still in uniform when I got off the bus and walked the few yards to their bungalow. My aunt recognised me straight away but my uncle as usual was gardening at a neighbours house.

"When he comes home say you are making enquiries about a watch that you believe he found in a garden, he won't recognise you in uniform"

He looked really worried as I questioned him formally and made notes, it was about ten minutes before he realised it was me and chased me round the garden with his spade. The drive back next day was uneventful but pleasant. Sometimes there is nothing to be on edge about, things going smoothly makes the job seem pleasant, but there is always an awareness that the unexpected may happen.

Often minor mishaps can be dealt with at the time, but the more persistent niggles occupy the mind and can become enlarged if allowed. Escort duties were a welcome break from the routine of prison life, an adventure from the drab existence of everyday sameness.

Transferring a prisoner to another prison or court with the responsibility for all involved was in direct contrast to the feeling of being a number in a huge organisation and just a turnkey.

CHAPTER 22
Detached Duty

I was given detached duty to Risley Remand Centre on compassionate grounds as both my parents were ill having suffered heart problems. Serving at Risley should have been a simpler task than at Wandsworth, the souths toughest no-nonsense nick. I arrived full of my own self-importance, undertaking any task or duty given to me. Risley besides being a remand centre was also a women's prison and a borstal.

One lunchtime I was given the task of keeping the borstal lads who were locked away quiet and to dissuade them from shouting obscenities from their windows across the to the women's prison. I was patrolling the landing on my own when I heard several youths shouting vulgarities to the women. I pinpointed an offending cell and unlocked the door. I should never unlock a door without any back up, but I was a tough screw from Wandsworth with experience of handling hardened criminals so any borstal lad would not present a problem. As soon as he heard the key in the lock he must have jumped on his bed. I was then the man in charge, swinging the door open I strolled in and gave him a lecture. He was apologetic enough and so I told him to stand up. He swung his legs off the bed and began to stand up, in fact he never stopped standing up; he was huge. I pointed my finger up to his face and told him to be quiet from now on or I would be back. "Most people think I'm thick because I'm a Geordie and am fairly big." I gave a sigh of relief as I hurriedly shut the door behind me.

A lesson learned; do not assume and do not overstate my own self-importance especially when the situation was of my own making.

CHAPTER 23
Wimbledon Hospice

I had a duty as a guard at Wimbledon Hospice, and was unsure as to what my responsibility would be, obviously to stop him from escaping. Not knowing what a hospice

The nurses were all beautiful and kind, generous with their time and unruffled. The contrast between here and a place a few miles down the road influenced me greatly. I calmly looked forward to each day with an assurance of positive vibes for the rest of my duty. The prisoner was making slow progress and becoming alive to his surroundings with a look of hope in his eyes. I finished my weeks guard duty; not surprised when I saw him a month later in the prison hospital, wearing a smile of recognition he nodded. Words were not necessary, a shared experience of how things could be was all that was needed.

I was back in the same routine again with a better understanding of life at both ends of the scale and how something so simple can affect my outlook. I became aware of my stress levels as they happened. It didn't change attitudes on the surface, I became more aware of myself and moderated my actions to suit the situation. Instead of reacting to stress, I began to respond accordingly.

CHAPTER 24
Regime Change

The Governor retired and was replaced by a more progressive authority who made gradual and subtle changes to the system. The entrenched attitudes prior to the new Governor taking his role were an unspoken no-nonsense, us and them, easy way or hard way practice.

Unchallenged by staff and prisoners, everyone knew where they stood. The old system was being dismantled slowly and not all changes were welcomed.

"If an officer tells me you were driving a motorcycle on the landing, I will believe him before I believe you." Is a quote from the retiring Governor.

"If an officer tells me you were driving a motorcycle on the landing, we will discuss the possibility of where you may have obtained the motorcycle." Is a quote from the new Governor.

Staff confidence and morale was dwindling, and discipline was eroding. Changes are not always accepted straight away and often need to be tested before being implemented. An uneasy restlessness between staff and Governor grade became a little strained, not undermined but with a healthy respect to resolve the differences. Prisoners became more vocal and confident, not demanding or threatening, still respectful but with a new voice they wanted to be heard and began to question and challenge certain rights they believed to which they were entitled.

The changes were more of attitude and less confrontational which encouraged a better understanding of the reality of prison life not seen before. The Chief officer retired and a Chief newly promoted from another prison took up the reins.

His authority was not accepted without some resistance from the staff; he was seen as a soft touch leaning towards the rights of prisoners than to the support of his staff.

Meetings were held by the P.O.A. (Prison Officers Association). Change was happening throughout the prison service 'out with the old and in with the new' was being resisted. New lighter blue uniforms, white shirts and name tags were expected within a few months and was considered too much at once by many.

CHAPTER 25
Mass Breakout Attempt

A good mate of mine Terry was astounded by some information he was given by a prisoner, he was suspicious of its content, but respected the prisoner who told him in absolute confidence fearing for his life.

"I don't know what to do" he said and so confided the facts to myself.

"There's going to be a mass breakout this summer" was all he knew, but he was gathering small bits of information as and when he could.

"Brixton is involved somehow, and it will be on a Wednesday." Over the next few days, I became involved and a clandestine letter from a prisoner in Brixton was intercepted by Terry with information stating a bin lorry running into the main gates at Brixton would be the signal for a breakout at Wandsworth.

We decided to write a report with what we knew and present it to the security P.O. A man full of his own self-importance, bluff and bluster. He dismissed the information with derision, suggesting that any security breaches he would know about before anyone else, he being head of security. To give him some credit he did report it to the governor who must have informed the Home Office as Terry was summoned to give his evidence to a bunch of suits at the home office.

This was becoming unbelievable and so we played it down, not knowing whether we were being used in some bizarre plot for someone's amusement or what if it happened. The 'snout', 'grass' or con with a conscience fed us what he knew as soon as he knew. Now it gets really beyond our imaginations as piece by piece we put together a picture that would be better used in a film thriller.

Welfare (civilian staff) with sensitive information about inmates families, would visit at lunchtime when prisoners were in their cells and whilst most of the staff were at lunch. One officer per wing was on duty who should be informed when non discipline staff were visiting; didn't always happen.

A gun would be used, smuggled in by a member of the farm party. An officer in the control room would delay sounding the alarm. All this seems far-fetched and distinctly unreal, but we had to follow where it led us. If there was a riot or disturbance at Brixton, staff from Wandsworth would respond to help quell any disturbance and vice-versa.

Last bit of the jigsaw was that a bin lorry arriving at Brixton would be hi-jacked by prisoners and would ram the gates signalling a riot. This was timed to happen during or just before lunch, staff from Wandsworth would respond leaving a skeleton staff manning the prison when most prisoners were 'banged up'.

Enter the female welfare officer visiting someone on D wing and the escape begins. What we assumed would follow was not backed up by intelligence received but by assumptions and logic. If the I.R.A. were involved, the ruthless determination and disregard for life was enough to send fear to the bravest of men. They were extremely active throughout London and major cities dispelling carnage wherever they planted their bombs.

The role of the terrorist forces was to attack the main entrance and force the gate staff to unlock the only barrier to their means of escape. The road at the entrance was a normal thoroughfare which was used by the general public at all times of the day. Cars could be parked, vans and trucks passed without any checks.

The whole escape plan though feasible was so incredibly daring, the enormity of it leaned toward the ridiculous and absurd and because of that had to be considered a risk. There's no more we can do, we don't know when it will happen or if it will happen although it would be a Wednesday, the refuse collection day at Brixton. We did not confide anything to our friends. The final report written and given to the Governor in early summer, was met with scepticism and the same amount of disbelief we both felt.

Nothing else could be done and so it was soon forgotten as prison routine and life carried on with its usual mini dramas and minor scuffles. A few weeks later on a Wednesday I was having a tea break in the mess and playing cards with Ted and Pete when Terry came bursting in shouting that the bin lorry at Brixton had rammed the gates. Alarmed as we all were a surge of excitement and incredulity along with a sense of 'we were right' surged through me.

The workshops were closed and the prison was in lockdown in rapid speed. All prisoners were banged up and a meeting was announced to happen in the admin building for all available staff. The Deputy governor informed all attending that a mass breakout may be attempted and that all precautions were being taken. Admin and welfare staff were to stay in their building and officers were to man the wings, the perimeter and to report anything suspicious.

I was given the perimeter road inside the prison and was surprised to see a helicopter hovering above, the sound of police sirens outside making themselves conspicuous and a sense of vindication for the hours we put in to gather the information. Letting the prisoners know that we were on to them was the best way to make it fail. I would like to say that Terry was given a special honour or at least a commendation.

Nothing was presented to either of us, a thank you for doing your job from the governor was the only reward. Wandsworth soon resumed its routine and any of the resulting punishments, transfers or losses of remission were not divulged. It would be simple to ascertain the prisoner who may have received a visit from welfare that day and to build a picture of his accomplices.

I was mystified as to why the after effects were not made public. The press reported the story as a false alarm and focussed on the bin lorry episode at Brixton. The consequences of the mass breakout could have possibly endangered many lives, if it had happened. The only proof we have is that a bin lorry did ram the gates at Brixton, that the prison was locked down in double quick time, a helicopter and police cars surrounded the prison. Terry and myself were left bewildered as to the lack of any further evidence from the powers that be about the incident. It was suspected that the I.R.A., Bahder Minjehoff and the Angry Brigade could have been involved. Ridiculous was the accepted assumption that flourished soon after the incident. This was the best way to end any speculation about any other outcome. What else did the Home Office know.? Playing it down was the best way of ignoring what could have been.

CHAPTER 26

Instances

No 1

A lot of happenings on their own were memorable and short lived, often humorous and sometimes a little frightening. The BBC programme Horizon gained Home Office approval to film inside Wandsworth, commenting on life behind bars. Mainly focussing on the routine and lives of prisoners, how well they were looked after and their rights as humans to a decent and healthy life.

A superficial and sanitized look at a system that was slowly changing. The lives of cons was becoming easier and a little more purposeful, the hierarchy amongst them becoming vociferous and questioning. Whilst they were filming, I was in charge of dinners on D wing when the producer asked me if he could try one of the sausage rolls being served to the prisoners. I told him, "If there are any left at the end of serving then I could let him you have one purely in the interest of social science and not because he was hungry." These rolls were massive, almost a foot long and a good two inches thick but looked so good. There were four left and so the producer picked one, as he started to bite into it the Centre P.O. appeared and barked in Sgt. Major style.

"What's that you're putting in your mouth sir."

He was so startled that he dropped it immediately giving the look of innocence I've seen so often. "Food is for prisoners only; would you like to become a prisoner Sir." The reply was most apologetic as he glared the 'glare' at myself as I smiled benignly.

Prunes were the dessert for that evening, dreaded by all staff left on duty which meant bells ringing for loo attention, at least until the night staff came on. Only two officers to a wing meant that the recesses (toilets) were used frequently as six at a time were unlocked from each wing. Fast acting was prunes; one prisoner was dragged off the loo by our only Cockney Screw who promptly sat in his place, sounding like Queen Mary coming in to port was a remark by his colleague. His hat and face visible above the reduced height door.

"Look at that written on the inside of the door, anything over a pound should be lowered, not dropped; nothing about pebble-dashing though. Limbo dancing banned."

Horizon left the building earlier, missing out on the reality of life in the raw. They couldn't put that in their programme and show it on a Wednesday evening.

Instance No 2

Prince of Darkness

K3 was my landing this particular day. I unlocked for slop out at breakfast and whilst everything ran smoothly went for my breakfast at 8.a. m.. Got back to the landing at 8.45. ready to unlock and turf them out to their workshops. Usual routine was to unlock one side of the landing and walk back checking the cells were empty and shutting the doors when I came across someone still in bed. He seemed sound asleep and was oblivious to my orders to get out of bed and to get to work. I tried shouting a bit louder, it didn't work. I then kicked the bed and removed his bed covers. Still no movement, he wasn't dead or unconscious as I could hear some sound coming from him and a slight movement from his head.

By now I was getting a bit impatient, so I filled a bucket full of water and went back to his cell. He was a man of African origin with tribal marks on his face. I yelled at him once more warning him I would pour the water over him if he didn't get up right away. No response other than he opened his eyes. I was becoming very irate, so I poured the water over his head expecting him to jump up immediately and rush to work. He was lay on his back as I emptied the bucket on him, his mouth was open slightly as he looked at the ceiling of his cell. I was amazed as he pursed his lips and blew out some of the water. No other movement whatsoever. I then became concerned that he may have been sick-in cell and excused work. Locking him in his cell I checked with the office and it confirmed that he arrived the previous evening,

80

having been convicted of committing aggravated burglary. His notes said he believed he was an African prince, unable to speak English and that he belonged to some voodoo sect. He must have been in a self-induced trance as he was still asleep when I checked on him later. I told the P.O. and left him to deal with it.

Instance No 3

Tears of Innocence

G2 landing; I was locking up and checking the count when I heard uncontrollable sobbing coming from a cell halfway along. It wasn't the sound of a regrettable cry, like someone who knew he'd done wrong and was feeling sorry for himself. It was a totally frustrating and regrettable cry of a man who was not ashamed of his tears. I asked him if he was o.k. and more tears flowed as he begged me to help him whilst claiming he was totally innocent of any crime. I usually take claims of innocence with a large helping of salt, but this was different, I tried to reassure him that British justice was fair and that he would get a chance to contest his conviction. Feeling tremendous sorrow for the man I instinctively believed him and wanted to help. I think I calmed him down enough for him to get some sleep.

When I came back on duty the next morning at 7 a.m he was packing up his bedroll and being taken to reception for release. He was the happiest man with a smile conveying his joy and relief as he thanked me profusely. I tried to convince him that I had no influence on the events and I guess he believed me; he was so exultant, thanking everyone he saw. That was a really good feel start to the day and a victory shared by all. It proved to me that not all prisoners were guilty of the crimes they were convicted of, that justice was sometimes unjust and, I like to think, rectified its mistakes.

Instance No 4

A Patchwork Rugby Team

Sport was a must for staff, it relieved tension created bonding and helped with fitness levels. Banter and friendly rivalry was a pre-requisite in any of the sports we tried; judo, Kendo, Karate, football, rugby, anything to prove our overall toughness and self -esteem. Basketball, cricket, volleyball and badminton were considered to be more gentle pursuits practiced by thinking men. Team sports of eleven or more were difficult to organise, rarely getting enough staff off duty at the same time and finding opponents who were prepared to play against the Screws. On a couple of occasions we did manage to get a rugby team together, mostly ex footballers a few ex-rugby players and some others we convinced were capable of passing a rugby ball. A real hotchpotch of misfits. Fifteen screws wearing shirts of different colours, different shorts, some wearing pumps and one wearing sandals.

Terry arranged a game against Surrey police on a Saturday and we managed to get a team together for that day. Hired a coach and set off for the Surrey ground. Intimidated a little as they warmed up in their bright yellow jerseys, passing the ball with ease, doing their stretches and weighing up the opposition with increasing confidence. Murmurings amongst our team and slightly bowed heads were noticeable, but not our resolve and determination.

In the clubhouse after the game, we celebrated a hard-won victory, and after most rugby games it is the friendliest place to be, no animosity, no vendettas or niggling criticisms and not too many regrets. They found it hard to believe that we had not played as a team prior to that day and congratulated us. Getting pissed and taking the piss was natural. Piling into the coach with our supporters and a few crates of beer we journeyed home. Singing, drinking, mooning at traffic and generally bragging about how good we played was soon accompanied by cries to stop the bus as soon as possible. On a stretch of the A3 in front of a hedge could be seen in the headlights of oncoming traffic a line of men watering the bushes. Except for one at the front who was suitably embarrassed having lights shining on his predicament. He hopped over the hedge and slipped into a ditch, full of mud he emerged after completing his task. He wasn't allowed back on the coach so he was 'persuaded' to complete the journey in the luggage compartment underneath; almost forgetting he was there when we arrived home. Aggression along with watching each other's backs was the winning formula for us that day, we were more afraid of them winning, than us losing.

Instance No. 5

B1 Fight

One morning on B1 whilst supervising the serving of breakfasts I heard a commotion behind me. I turned and saw two prisoners in a scuffle; one was considerably older whilst the younger looked as if he could handle himself. Without thinking I stepped in between them and pulled the older man away. He was so irate and intent on landing a punch that I raised my hand to stop him getting too close while still holding on to the other man. The old man walked straight into my hand and was flung backwards. I didn't push him or use any force, but he hit the stone floor with the back of his head; seeing blood oozing from the impact made my stomach turn over, with the fear I had killed him. I panicked and yelled for hospital staff who soon appeared, gave immediate first aid and took him to hospital. Fortunately, he was deemed fit after a week in hospital, my fear and dread abated. Such a terrifying ordeal to feel responsible for the apparent death of someone even if by accident. Don't interfere in a fight between inmates until it is over was sound advise given in hindsight.

CHAPTER 27
Transfer to Strangeways

The year is 1974 and after five years of working at Wandsworth, with all the happenings, events and experiences I failed to notice the strain it was putting on my marriage. My wife was insistent on travelling to Manchester whenever she could to visit her family which added more stress. She eventually left and returned to her family. This was a heartbreaking period for us both and to cut a long story short I was eventually given a transfer to Strangeways, to hopefully restore our marriage. For various reasons this did not happen and so I no longer needed that secure job. I decided to face the outside world and learn new skills.

CHAPTER 28
Opinion

My five-year stint as a discipline officer was eye-opening, humorous, and often scary. I learned the difference between bravado and bravery, stupidity and common sense, whilst making some great friends. Not everyone who wore a navy uniform could be trusted and not everyone who wore prison grey was untrustworthy. Riots were unheard of, unrest was rare. Having seen many changes in the prison service during my short term, when I first joined there was no association, no radios, no gymnasium. Prisoners were given by right a health system, a balanced and nutritious diet, regular work, medical attention and a local shop. Everything they needed was available, including the right and accommodation to practice their particular religion.

The changes that were made in my last couple of years were supposedly progressive and humane. It seemed that whilst the changes made in respect of prisoners was foremost; the progression, consideration and working conditions for staff was non-existent.

The cooperation of prisoners will always be needed to run a prison, the morale and efforts made by staff to maintain that trust must be recognized and rewarded. Looking at it simply, improving conditions for prisoners without improving staff conditions will create an unstable atmosphere. You can't give to one without giving to the other and still expect the status quo. That's how the system begins to fail.

Inmates in the majority are 'inside' for a variety of reasons, mostly for trying to buck the system and get something for nothing; so when given something they don't have to strive for, or pay for, or earn they will ask for more and like unruly children kick up a fuss until they get what they want. There was hardly any unrest in Wandsworth, very little was given in the way of privileges e.g. association, gymnasium, radios or television. All their needs were met and although discipline was thought to be strict they knew where they stood. The only thing that needed to be improved was the toileting facilities.

The gangland families who ran the criminal underworld were being replaced by a more subtle type of thug. Corporate criminality was arriving. A better educated criminal who could articulate his needs with words, not threats. The Krays, Richardsons and Tibbs being replaced by syndicated crime.

My resignation was timely.

Author Ron Kendrick

.